Harrie Tubm

D1251727

Teri L. Tilwick

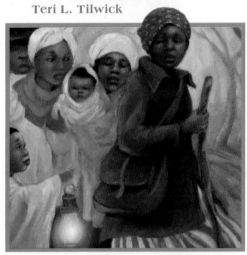

Boston, Massachusetts
Chandler, Arizona
Glenview, Illinois
Upper Saddle River, New Jersey

Illustrations
Opener, 1, 3, 5, 6, 7, 8, 9, 10, 11, 12, 13, 14 Susan Cornelison.

Photographs
Every effort has been made to secure permission and provide appropriate credit for photographic material.
The publisher deeply regrets any omission and pledges to correct errors called to its attention in subsequent editions.

Unless otherwise acknowledged, all photographs are the property of Pearson Education, Inc.

Photo locators denoted as follows: Top (T), Center (C), Bottom (B), Left (L), Right (R), Background (Bkgd)

All Photos: Library of Congress.

ISBN-13: 978-0-328-67593-7
ISBN-10:   0-328-67593-8

3 4 5 6 V0FL 16 15 14 13 12

She hid in the dark behind trees. She escaped from **slavery**. This is the story of brave Harriet Tubman.

Harriet was born into slavery. Her grandparents were from West Africa.

Harriet lived on a large **plantation** in Maryland. Edward Brodess owned it. Slaves helped grow corn and wheat.

Slaves had no rights. They could not learn to read. Harriet's father worked in the fields. He taught her about nature. He taught her useful things.

Harriet learned of the Underground Railroad. This was not a kind of train. It was a secret way to escape slavery.

An **overseer** chased a runaway slave. Harriet stood in front of the slave. The overseer hit her in the head. She had many headaches after that.

Harriet married John Tubman. She wanted them both to run away. He did not want to go.

One day, Harriet did escape. She followed the Underground Railroad. She went to a kind woman's home. The woman told her where to go next.

Harriet was brave. She traveled for three weeks. She crossed into Pennsylvania. There was no slavery there.

Harriet was happy to be free. Still, she missed her family and friends.

Harriet returned to lead her sister to freedom. She made many more trips.

Harriet's parents could not walk far. She helped them escape in a wagon.

Harriet helped 300 slaves get to freedom. She made 19 trips in all.

Harriet was a spy in the Civil War.
She helped newly freed slaves.

Harriet later lived in New York. She helped people there, too. We think of her as an American hero. She was a remarkable woman.

Glossary

overseer person in charge of slaves

plantation large farm

slavery being owned by others and
  forced to work without pay